OREGON COAST

OREGON COAST

PHOTOGRAPHY BY

RAY ATKESON

TEXT BY

ARCHIE SATTERFIELD

CONTENTS

International Standard Book Number 0-912856-06-8
Library of Congress Catalog Card Number 75-188295
Copyright © 1972 by publisher Charles H. Belding
Designer Robert Reynolds
Printer Graphic Arts Center
Bindery Lincoln & Allen
Printed in the United States of America
Third Printing

PREFACE

My introduction to the Oregon Coast was a camping trip with some friends in 1928, shortly after I had migrated to the Northwest from Kansas City. I knew or cared little of the historical significance of our coastline, nor did I realize that I was enjoying the privilege of seeing one of the most magnificent stretches of coastline in the world; however that first visit was an experience never forgotten.

Today's Oregon Coast is a far cry from that which we explored that year. Changes, both good and bad, have transpired since then. In 1928, motorists were conspicuous by their absence, roads were poor and provided limited access to only a few seashore areas. Probably half of the coastline was roadless, or if the roads existed, they were virtually impassable for passenger cars. Numerous bays and inlets, both large and small, dictated miles of inland detours or transportation by ferry. Even the stretches of highway that were drivable were dirt or corduroy.

Corduroy roads were an early-day engineering marvel of the Northwest, most prevalent in areas of more or less constant mud. There were miles of corduroy, consisting of thick planks or rough-hewn timber cut barely long enough for the width of the wheels of trucks and cars. The planks were laid side by side in the dirt to simulate as closely as possible a smooth roadbed. With the passage of time, some planks decayed or sank in the mud, necessitating constant repairs. The result was very rough and slow travel.

The highlight of that initial trip was a few days of camping on the peninsula between Depoe Bay and Boiler Bay. The latter, now a state park, was named for an old iron boiler that washed up into the bay from a ship which was wrecked in a storm in 1910. The boiler is still there, where it has withstood the ravages of time and the sea.

Depoe Bay, a picturesque forest-bound cove with a narrow, twisting lava channel connection to the sea, forced one of our many inland detours. One of the earliest of several beautifully designed bridges was later stretched across the deep channel to carry highway traffic. Others since have been built across rivers and bays to create links in the three-hundred-mile highway chain along the Oregon Coast.

During our encampment there, we spent days watching the crashing surf, exploring tidal caves and tunnels, searching a tiny agate-strewn beach and swimming in an underground lake which we never had the courage to thoroughly explore. We patronized the single small store and gas pump near the bay, seeking refuge and warmth from the open stove after being drenched by rain.

Now Depoe Bay is one of the busiest and most picturesque deep-sea fishing havens on the entire Pacific Coast. The harbor depth has been dredged and charter, commercial and private boats constantly squirm through the narrow channel to and from the sea during the summer season, thrilling spectators who line the highway bridge that arches across the channel. Numerous stores, restaurants, souvenir shops, an aquarium and modern motels line the highway on both sides of the bay for a mile. The highway and large parking area are jammed to capacity on weekends and even on weekdays during summer months. When the sea is rough, sightseers can enjoy a close-up view of the famed spouting horn that sometimes showers people and cars on the highway. Homes now cover the peninsula where we spent several days of solitude. (Sometimes I wonder if those residents are aware of the lake and tidal caves beneath them.) A short path leads to a point on the lava cliffs where the surf often stages spectacular shows. Unfortunately, a picturesque offshore sandstone arch rock was destroyed several years ago by the relentless sea, and I doubt if many agates that once were so plentiful can be found now on the small beach beside the highway.

Boiler Bay State Park has become a favorite sightseeing and picnic spot where visitors watch the crashing surf that sometimes explodes high above the cliffs. The once thriving and beautiful marine gardens, exposed during low tide for intimate viewing, have been virtually destroyed by thoughtless specimen collectors. Oil has occasionally washed ashore from passing ships and contributed to the extinction of some marine life in the tidal pools.

In my opinion, Cape Kiwanda on the Northern Coast, is the most photogenic square mile of coastline in America. It is a favorite rendezvous for photographers and sightseers from all points of the nation. Many prize-winning color photos of spectacular surf and shoreline action there have rewarded both amateur and professional cameramen.

The earliest photos I saw of Kiwanda were taken by two amateur photographer friends. Their photos (black-and-whites taken about 1930) were so artistically beautiful that I was lured to those colorful sandstone cliffs soon afterward. I believe it is safe to say that since then, I've visited Kiwanda more times, shot more commercial-size film than any other photographer. Sad to relate, I've also probably discarded more poor pictures of the area than any other photographer. The place is so exciting when conditions of surf and lighting are favorable that I am still unable to resist the temptation to shoot more and more throw-away pictures. Occasionally, one is sufficiently attractive to find its way into print.

For many years, the cape was a considerable hiking distance from Pacific City. Then an access road reached to within a quarter of a mile of the south side of the cape, requiring only a short scramble up and over sand dunes to reach the most photogenic area. That approach was shortened by an access incline, down which visitors and fishermen by the thousands could drive onto the beach directly to the foot of the cliffs during summer low tides.

Beach driving at Kiwanda and other popular beaches eventually reached a saturation point, and during summer months only special-purpose vehicles such as boat-launching trailers are permitted access to the beach. So we're back to the quarter-mile hike again. Vehicles are also subject to restrictions on most other Oregon beaches during summer months.

A word of caution is in order here: Wet sandstone cliffs become slick and surf action can be dangerous. Several lives have been lost at Kiwanda resulting from carelessness.

Yes, the Oregon Coast has undergone some great changes since I first visited it in 1928. For many years, a fine paved highway has skirted the Pacific from the Columbia River to the California state line. Long stretches of it has been modernized, and in many places relocated for the heavy and speedier traffic of today. Other areas are undergoing modernization, and some stretches are sorely in need of relocation to by-pass congested resort areas.

Unfortunately, coastal-resort development, with several outstanding exceptions—has been unplanned or poorly planned. Too little consideration has been given environmental problems. Some coastal communities are cluttered with unsightly structures. Balance of nature on some estuaries and other areas has been destroyed. Magnificent forests have disappeared before the saw, axe and fires. Even nature has had a hand in destruction of isolated forest areas as violent storms sweep in from the Pacific.

No longer can we drive through virgin forests of giant evergreens. A few "see-through" corridors of old-growth timber have been left along highways crossing the Coast Range, and a few impressive forest stretches may still be enjoyed on the Oregon Coast Highway. The most outstanding example of the great forests that once covered the western slopes of the Coastal Mountains still crowns the dome of Cascade Head. Unlike many other promontories overlooking Oregon's shoreline which have been scalped by civilization's progress, Cascade Head boasts a luxuriant growth of timber that covers hundreds of acres. Travelers on the relocated coast highway which sweeps in gentle curves up over the eastern shoulder of this wilderness-like domain catch glimpses of the forests that reach across to the precipitous cliffs which drop abruptly to inaccessible shore-line coves. Unfortunately, areas of virgin forests are too few and too small, serving only as a brief illusion of past beauty.

The illusion is lessened by the "see-through" character of some corridors which permit screened views of the destruction that lies beyond. To the credit of modern controlled logging practice, more effort is being directed toward reforestation than in the earlier years of timber harvest along the coast and in the Coast Range. Most of these scars left by logging and forest fires have been partially healed with alder and salal growth, both of which unfortunately are so dominant that reforestation with evergreen trees for the future is practically impossible. One outstanding exception is the site of the infamous Tillamook Burn area in the Coast Range, where more than four hundred thousand acres of virgin timber was destroyed in two of the greatest holocausts of modern history in the early 1930s.

The fires resulted from a combination of man's carelessness followed by dry, searing east winds which fanned the flames and carried smoke toward the sea, where it darkened coastal communities and deposited ashes on ships fifty miles off the coast. The disaster is still vivid in the memories of Oregonians who were living in the region at the time.

I recall a harrowing first-hand description of the fire, told by an elderly gentleman who had a remote home on the Salmon-berry River that was a popular rendezvous for fishermen.

He had been trapped in the heart of the fire, imprisoned for days. His home, of course, was destroyed and he was forced to spend several hours in a deep pool in the river with the inferno raging all around, burning snags crashing nearby, and a congestion of wild animals, including cougar, bear, deer, elk and raccoons, sharing the sanctuary of the pool with him, all with only one thought—preservation of life. The heat was so intense the old gentleman's hair and face were badly singed. Some animals died when the water and air temperature became unbearable for them. Thousands perished elsewhere in the inferno.

Earlier I mentioned that the Tillamook Burn was a forestry exception. More than a decade after the disaster, the State Forestry Department and timber industries built access roads into the rugged mountain terrain, salvaged all possible snags left standing until it was practical to reseed the area by helicopter and manpower. Many acres were replanted by school children from Portland, Tillamook and other communities. Those children, like my daughter, are grown now and have children of their own. They can be justifiably proud when they drive across the Coast Range via the Sunset Highway or Wilson

River Highway. Once again, young evergreen forests are thriving in thousands of acres of the devastated area.

We can thank the late Sam Boardman, "Father of Oregon's State Parks," and his successors for preserving and developing some of the finest scenic beauty and natural attractions in more than eighty state and wayside parks along the coastal area.

I once had an enjoyable hike through Silver Falls State Park in the foothills of the Cascade Range with Mr. Boardman, and I was impressed with his visionary and enthusiastic discussion of our state park system. It was with some surprise that I learned from him that his favorite of all the state reserves in Oregon to that date was Honeyman Park on the central Oregon Coast. As I have become more familiar with the park, I can now understand his special devotion to it. I'm sure he would have worked diligently to preserve the surrounding coastal sand dunes as a national seashore park or as a national recreation area.

Sam Boardman was a great man, to whom we and future generations owe a tremendous debt of gratitude.

Other than relocation of highways, the Cannon Beach area on the North Coast has undergone less drastic changes than one might expect, considering its accessibility and popularity. A magnificent state park, Ecola, was developed a few miles north of Cannon Beach on land acquired in 1932. Here was a forest-bound parking and picnic area with a small grass-bordered lakelet nearby, where a herd of elk and several deer browsed in the evening, undisturbed by people. The elk later disappeared, as the story is told, when "sportsmen" drove them out of the park into a nearby logged area where other "sports-men" with guns decimated the herd. True or not, the herd suddenly disappeared. A few deer still graze contentedly beside the picnic area or on the steep slopes above the surf.

Several years ago, after the forests were logged from surrounding hillsides, a great slide of rain-soaked land swept toward the sea, taking with it the original parking area, lake, comfort station, the surrounding forest and picnic facilities. A larger parking and picnic area with a network of trails skirting headlands and beaches have since been developed to again create a beautiful park. But gone is the sylvan atmosphere of the dense forest and tiny lake. Nevertheless, it is one of the most popular of the coastal parks.

As we have become more conscious of the importance of preserving the balance of our ecology, we can already see some improvements in planning for future development along the Oregon Coast, as is the case in many other areas of America. I hope that more and more people who live here or visit our coast will be able to view with pride the results of man's co-operation with nature to preserve the good things we have. And I hope they will strive to improve the environment which some have so thoughtlessly helped to destroy.

In spite of past indiscretions and attacks on nature, the Oregon Coast has managed to survive as one of the world's most magnificent shorelines. Many scars of timber harvest and fire destruction are recovering with the help of Mother Nature, who works overtime in this environment of plentiful rain and a mild year-around climate.

Perhaps this book and its photos chosen, with a few exceptions, to emphasize the natural wonders of our coastal area, will cause more people to take a second and more appreciative look at the treasure we have. It is ours to improve and protect for the future.

RAY ATKESON

Breakers explode in thundering fury against
sandstone cliffs of Shore Acres State Park.

Sunlight shines through a leaping wave revealing a translucent beauty in the tempestuous surf.

The Oregon Dunes National Recreation
Area created by Congressional action in 1972
includes more than 32,000 acres of coastal
dunes which are unique in contrasting
character. Picturesque pools and islands of
vegetation are surrounded by vast expanses
of shifting sand.

The sun sinks behind an incoming cloud
bank as vacationists enjoy surf and sand at
Beverley Beach State Park.

Moisture jewels decorate intricately woven
spider webs in marshes along the Lewis and
Clark River and the sun bursts in a blaze of
glory from behind shoreline trees of a coastal
stream as autumn ground fog melts away.

Early morning autumn mists veil
coastal mountains towering above a
Tillamook County dairy farm.

Luminous clouds, remnants of a Pacific
storm front, pour their moisture into the sea
as the late afternoon sun spreads its glow
in the clearing atmosphere.

A small shorebird scurries along the sand
at sunset as gentle surf pushes a fringe of
foam in close pursuit.

THE NORTHERN COAST

Biological historians tell us the first frontier crossed by living creatures was from the darkness of the sea womb into the land's hostile surface, and that it happened so many million of years ago that the species known as *homo sapiens* has not been in existence long enough to constitute a blink in time's eye. If these things are true (how can we ever be absolutely certain?), it helps explain that powerful attraction we feel for the coastline; the need to return to that first frontier where, for reasons which probably will always be shrouded in mystery, organisms chose a completely new environment. There are those among us who believe our attraction to the sea is in part the result of a primeval attitude stored in our genes, a memory transmitted down the millennia from a time the sea was a religious symbol for an inarticulated belief.

While the shape is always changing, sometimes subtly and other times dramatically, there is a permanency to the shoreline that offers comfort in a world where man appears intent upon changing the whole face of the planet. This mysterious frontier where land and sea meet offers a relief from unwanted, artificial change. The sea continues its unending assault against the rocks and the beaches, slowly, patiently wearing them down and reshaping them. The land retaliates by stretching long fingers of silt and sand out from estuaries, building bars and spits and peninsulas.

The infrequent visitor to the coast does not notice this nor is it what he usually is there for. He is there to look at it and listen to it at night, to walk along its edge beneath the seagull's cry and to experience the sunsets and to turn his back temporarily on the land and its problems. Here he can stand facing the west in the worst of winter storms and feel at ease, although he might not be able to tell you why.

Of all the coastline on North America's western shore, it is the Oregon Coast which seems best designed and managed for man to enjoy. Its beauty has resulted in millions of words, to which these can be added, beginning with the first explorers from Spain, England and Russia. Each ship's captain, while making laborious notations in his ship's log with mildew creeping inward from the edges, alternately spoke of scurvy among his crew and the coastal beauty. The view from pitching decks simply could not be ignored.

Overland explorers followed the same pattern. Even though the Lewis and Clark party spoke of hordes of fleas, "pore" meat and Indians with a different code of conduct than they were accustomed to, the explorers also spoke frequently of the beauty surrounding their stinking, damp winter quarters in 1805-06.

The area of most intense activity early in Oregon's coastal history was around the mouth of that great river highway of the west, the Columbia River. Five years after Lewis and Clark departed for home, John Jacob Astor established an ill-fated fur empire there. The empire perished, but not the town founded and named for him. Although it is several miles from the coast, Astoria definitely is a coastal, sea-going town. Brackish water sweeps back and forth in front of the busy port, stopping and reversing the swift flow of the mighty river, exposing and then covering mudflats seen from the four-mile-long Astoria-Megler Bridge which links Oregon and Washington.

On both sides of the Columbia's broad estuary are the jetties, excellent examples of manmade attempts to infringe upon the sea, and the resulting natural law of compensation. The Columbia River bar, long known as the "Graveyard of the Pacific," was littered with the broken remains of vessels forced aground by storms during virtually every decade since its discovery in 1792 by Captain Robert Gray. Long fingers of boulders were stretched out into the ocean on either side of the river to improve navigation across the savage bar. But their presence caused eddies which collect sand and silt, moving the high tide mark farther and farther west each year, forming high dunes that conceal the sea from homes and motels along the original beach.

One of the scores of ships to perish here was the Peter Iredale, a beautiful, 2,075-ton British bark which ran aground in 1906. Part of its iron-clad hulk remains on the beach, but is slowly being covered by sand and eaten away by rust. It is one feature of the most popular of the coast's state parks. Although Fort Stevens State Park is not the largest or the most convenient or even the most beautiful of the string of parks running from the northern to southern border of the state, it is the most heavily used and one of the few with overnight camping facilities to remain open the year around.

The matter of Oregon's coastal parks is an intriguing one and the envy of other coastal states around the country. The history of them is a story of a happy accident and deep wisdom on the part of public officials and their appointed employees. And to further simplify a situation other states have been unable to resolve, the parks are tied inexorably with the award-winning Highway 101, which runs the length of the coast, for the most part complementing rather than interfering with the scenery.

Until the first decade of this century, the principal coastal transportation system was the beach, with an occasional ferry across larger streams and corduroy roads through swamps and over headlands jutting out into the ocean. Anxious to protect this natural thoroughfare, but not yet interested in parks, the state in 1913 under the leadership of Governor Oswald West, declared the beaches public highways.

It wasn't until 12 years later that the state began thinking in terms of parks along the coast. When this occurred the state found, to its pleasant surprise, that it already owned the finest stretch of parkland on the West Coast. Immediately a vigorous acquisition campaign was begun to put the major headlands and other dominant features under public ownership. Then, in the 1950s, another acquisition program began, this time to acquire the lower, flatter stretches of ocean front property for campgrounds. This has been bolstered over the years by generous gifts of property and sales, many at below-market prices.

Consequently, the public owns all the beaches and more than half of the 362 miles of ocean frontage back of the high-tide line. You won't see signs banning you from *these* beaches or "For Sale" signs as you will in neighboring states. In fact, you can be certain you've left Oregon when you see the first sign advertising ocean frontage for sale.

Recognizing both the beauty of the coast and the heavy traffic it brings, the state has developed more than 80 parks and waysides along its length, roughly one-third of its vast park system. Add to this the Forest Service, Bureau of Land Management and other governmental agencies' parks spotted along the coast, and it is doubtful any 350-mile stretch of coastline in the world is better designed for man to enjoy. There are people who have been visiting the coast regularly for decades and have yet to see everything the parks have to offer. No lifetime is long enough to do so.

It is thus with Fort Stevens State Park and the others within sight and sound of the surf as one heads south on a modern, comfortable voyage of discovery. The best preparation for such an undertaking is to fully equip yourself with brochures from the Oregon State Highway Division, the Oregon Coast Association and chambers of commerce along the way. While brochures are to be digested with a dash of salt (there *are* cloudy, rainy days in this paradise), they can be trusted for basic information.

At this writing no interpretive sign graces Battery Russell, near Fort Stevens State Park, and one should. It was the only military establishment in the U. S. to be fired upon by the Japanese during World War II. The battery wisely did not return the fire—its old 10 inch disappearing rifles provided a very limited range—and the Japanese submarine's shots were wide of their mark. Local enterprising youngsters capitalized on the event by breaking up an old cast-iron stove and selling chunks of "Japanese shrapnel" to the inevitable curiosity seekers the following day.

Inland a few miles is the replica of Lewis and Clark's winter quarters, Fort Clatsop National Memorial, with an interpretive center and picnic areas. It is one of the few forts where no shots were fired in anger.

Down the broad, open beach a few miles is the coast's oldest resort area. There are grandparents who vividly recall spending their childhood summers in Seaside and Gearhart, just as there are youngsters today who feel their summer is incomplete without a visit to the two towns separated geographically by the curving Necanicum River and philosophically by the quiet life opposed to the festive.

Brooding over these extremes is the first major headland on the coast south of the Columbia — Tillamook Head, tall, storm-swept and dark with timber which often is dripping with rain and fog. A trail leads over the top of the head to Ecola State Park, and if you do not tarry, it is possible to walk around its base during extreme low tides. If, however, you are caught in one of the "death traps," those *cul-de-sacs* against the perpendicular cliffs, you will stay there watching the surf advance at you, or until a Coast Guard helicopter from Hammond plucks you to safety. A mile offshore stands the remains of Tillamook Rock Lighthouse, one of the loneliest outposts devised by man, and a stay in one of the "death traps" will give you a kinship with the men who served on the rock until its closure in the 1950s.

The southern side of the head is occupied by Ecola State Park, and it is here that the character of the coast dramatically changes. Offshore rocks break the monotony of long, barren beaches, and for the rest of the journey southward there will always be offshore rocks, or sea stacks, in view. Many of the rocks have been declared federal bird refuges and it is illegal to climb them.

Hard against Tillamook Head is Indian Beach, a place that is synonymous with surfing. Here the young, and young at heart, don wet suits for protection against the cold water and find some of the best wave "sets" on the coast. It isn't California or Hawaii surfing, but it suffices.

It is the heads and the capes and the points that dominate both the scenery and the imagination. There are Cape Falcon and Neahkahnie Mountain where the highway south of Cannon Beach takes traffic above the low fog that often hugs the shore and exposes only the tips of Haystack and other offshore rocks. Below the fog the mystery of Neahkahnie and its treasure and the chunks of beeswax from some unnamed wrecked ship tempt and tantalize treasure hunters and historians.

The mountain, graced by Oswald West State Park, conjures up images of pirates, plunder and murders by the light of flickering lanterns. Contrast this grim scene with the delightful stroll from the parking lot beside the highway to Short Sand Beach, or to the overnight campground, both only yards from the highway but light years away from its asphalt characteristics. The vision of pirates fades....

Buildings along the coast age gracefully, especially those whose owners have ignored the pleas of paint salesmen. One sees homes of all ages along the coast, but it is those aging wooden ones, cured in the storms and hard sunlight until they blend with driftwood, that reflect the character of beach living. As you skirt Nehalem and Tillamook Bay before heading inland to Tillamook, you will see these homes and motels off the highway. There's an honesty to them; they look established and more in place than many of the ultramodern, service-station architectural styles brought in by urban-oriented architects and land developers.

Tillamook. Glossy-coated dairy cattle grazing in the early morning fog. Elephantine World War II blimp hangars, one housing a sawmill. World-famous cheese. The surprise of a natural-history museum worthy of a large city presided over by a peppery octogenarian named Alex Walker. Short side trips up into the Coast Range where tree skeletons serve as monuments to the Tillamook Burn and elegant waterfalls soar down the cliffs toward the sea. But don't forget the coast, and you will if you don't study the map. Turn off the main highway and head west again, along Tillamook Bay to Cape Meares.

There's an abandoned lighthouse out at Cape Meares and a more practical but less romantic automated one nearby. In the evening you'll hear shorebirds chattering into the darkness and see cottontail rabbits crossing your path. A lesson in the uncertain relationship between the sea and land plants is taught by the Octopus Tree, a contorted spruce that survived the ocean storms only by drastically changing its shape, growing individual branches rather than the single, missile-straight trunk common to its species.

At the northern foot of the cape, at the townsite of Cape Meares, one sees the dead and dying trees, killed by the surf as it slowly moved into the resort town of Bayocean when the first Tillamook Bay jetty was built. The current's new course also undermined a large resort, which was abandoned shortly before it collapsed into the sea. Now, with the second jetty built, the current apparently has returned to its original course and the sand is slowly being replaced.

At this writing, the area from Tillamook south to Cascade Head is a region of controversy. It has the common elements: highway relocation and land use, to build or not to build and where. Much of the area in question has remained relatively untouched, if one ignores hillsides denuded of timber and Netarts Bay's face changing for real estate and boat basin development. The views from the headlands of Cape Lookout, Cape Kiwanda and Cascade Head acquire a monetary value for their timber and views; the small, delicate estuaries Netarts and Nestucca become potential marinas in the eyes of their beholders. Nature becomes a piece of merchandise rather than a birthright.

Some advocate harvesting, or at the least, thinning timber on these virgin headlands, but there is no natural or man-made law prohibiting the wind from blowing down trees occasionally as it has done for centuries. Nor is there any law stating that every square inch of beach and riverbank must have a monetary value. Since spiritual and aesthetical values must be experienced and cannot be measured by a calculator or stored in a computer's memory bank, it is virtually impossible for proponents of one philosophy to negotiate with the other.

But consider the geological miracle that is Cape Kiwanda. At one time it was a sandy beach, then it sank beneath the ocean and the multicolored sand was compressed into stone. Then, Lazarus-like, it rose from the sea and became the stunning cliffs we see today. The sandstone carved through the centuries by wind and surf never looks the same two days in a row. Like many objects of great beauty, there is an element of danger to be considered when hiking around the cliffs; when they are wet, they are extremely slick, and should one fall in, they are almost impossible to climb onto from the sea. Life rings anchored to posts by long lines have been installed, but they are repeatedly stolen by vacant-minded people who do not realize that in so doing, they are potentially guilty of manslaughter.

Safety on the beaches and in boats has become a major problem on the coast. Each year the Coast Guard's list of emergency calls grows longer, and too often they find only an overturned boat or a lifeless form on the beach. Applied common sense would prevent most tragedies.

If you visit the cape when the commercial fishermen are working, prepare yourself for excitement. They launch their swift Kiwanda dories into the surf and sometimes take them 50 to 60 miles to sea in pursuit of albacore when the salmon aren't running. Their return is spectacular. They roar directly at the shore slapping the throttle back at the last moment and hoisting the inboard-outboard engines. Then they run right up on the beach, high and dry. One cannot help but compare them with Vikings or longboat Indians. The dories are so versatile that, like coals to Newcastle, they are being sent to Samoa for use there.

From here to Newport the coast is something of a mixed bag. There are a series of state parks and waysides as beautiful and varied as will be found in any 30 miles in the world. On either side of the highway is a conglomeration of amusement parks, restaurants, cafes, motels, gift shops, grocery stores, etc. It is known as Lincoln City, or the "Twenty Miracle Miles," honestly and intentionally designed to attract tourists and their money. Like much of the Northern Coast, it is often controversial and a nightmare for planners charged with satisfying business and environmental interests. Local businessmen have an irrefutable argument in their favor: If people didn't like the atmosphere, they wouldn't come. They do come, in droves from the inland, and enjoy the carnival atmosphere and the crowds that mill around the highway's border.

Obviously there are many people who do not like solitude, and the thought of going to the coast, or anywhere else, without having people near them all the time is incomprehensible. The Oregon Coast from Lincoln City to Newport is designed for such people. Not only is it crowded with people on the streets and on the beaches, it also is an area of varied and closely packed natural beauty. There are some seven state parks, seven towns, a lighthouse and uncounted places to stop for a brief look at some natural or man-made feature.

Such land-use problems prove the need for coordinated planning on the entire coast. Obviously it can't be entirely wilderness or entirely urban, but its natural beauty must be protected or its commercial value will decrease.

The Northern Coast culminates at Newport, a charming port town with one of the most beautiful bridges in Oregon swooping over Yaquina Bay. The Oregon State University's oceanographic center here has made Newport something of a scientific center for the coast. Research into the continental shelf, the commercial fishing industry and the ocean currents have been supplemented by community involvement. The center's scientists have been active and effective in drawing attention to the problems faced by planners for the coastal estuaries. The center's recommendations were largely responsible for the widely hailed Yaquina Bay zoning ordinances, the most sensible land-use policy adopted for a coastal estuary to date.

The problems of other Oregon Coast estuaries remain unsolved, but with the creation of the Seashore Environmental and Development Council, the problem may be moving toward solution. Some coastal interests greeted the council with less than enthusiasm, but time and use will undoubtedly wear off the rough edges, permitting the council to work for the best interests of the greatest number of people.

A sea-going ship glides beneath the interstate
bridge which spans the mighty Columbia
River between the historic port of Astoria
and the state of Washington. Beyond the
city, Youngs Bay and tidal flats of Youngs
River reach toward Saddle Mountain
in the Coast Range.

The Oregon Coast Highway, U.S. 101, is linked by a number of attractively designed bridges. Here graceful arches reach across Yaquina Bay, Coos Bay, and the Rogue River.

Surf-combed seagrass clings to lichen-
covered marine garden rocks at Boiler Bay
State Park.

Autumn's artistry is displayed at its best
in the Coast Range where vine maple foliage
mingles with a young forest of evergreens.

The mountains meet the sea at Cannon Beach and Ecola State Park. A winter storm drapes a blanket of snow on the higher mountains, probably simulating conditions that existed when members of the Lewis and Clark party traveled over Tillamook Head to this point during their winter encampment at Fort Clatsop.

A deer silhouetted above the surf at Ecola
State Park seems to be enthralled by the
beauty of a colorful sunset.
Foxglove and salal are among the most
commonly seen blossoms along the coast, and
vine maple foliage in the Coast Range is
vividly colorful in autumn.

The autumn season is perhaps the
most fascinating of any on the Oregon
Coast. This sunrise panorama from
the trail on Tillamook Head encompasses
Indian Beach, Ecola Park, and Cannon
Beach, veiled beneath a blanket of fog at
the foot of coastal mountains.

Pennants of moss sway gracefully from
an evergreen bough as a spot of sunshine
finds its way into forest depths.

Early spring foliage begins to show on a
native maple cloaked in a heavy robe of club
moss, which is characteristic of rain forest
conditions that exist along the coastal
foothills.

The Oregon Coast Highway skirts
daringly along precipitous cliffs
of Neahkahnie Mountain where vista
points permit travelers opportunities to
pause and enjoy spectacular views.

A leisurely trail hike to the top of
Neahkahnie Mountain unfurls a rewarding
panorama of beaches, headlands, and the
Nehalem estuary.

A flock of sanderlings play tag with incoming
surf as waves lash the cliffs of Cape Lookout
which extends far out past the beach at
Cape Lookout State Park.

A popular nature trail, featuring old growth
forests and spectacular views, penetrates
a dense grove of small spruce trees on the
fog-bound crest of Cape Lookout.

Marshy meadows of coastal dairy pastures
and streams are a favorite habitat of this spring
flowering plant. Because of an unpleasant
odor, it bears the disparaging but appropriate
name of Skunk Cabbage.

Early morning sunburst through picturesque
fog-veiled shoreline trees mirrored on the
tranquil tidal water of the Tillamook River.

Driftwood is a coastal commodity that
is not likely to be rationed. It is produced in
great quantity and in many ways. It may be
hewn by surf, sand and rocks from thousands
of logs which reach the sea. Or, as in this
area, near Cape Meares, the sea is carving the
shoreline and capturing uprooted trees in
its angry clutches, eventually to be sculptured
into many driftwood treasures for fortunate
beachcombers.

An arch rock stands with other "stacks"
above a sandy beach at Oceanside.

Cape Kiwanda's moods are as varied as
surf action that lashes its sandstone cliffs.
Changes of light, with movement of
clouds and sun combine with restless
surf to make this cne of the most
photogenic coastal areas in the world.

Backwash from a receding wave meets an
incoming breaker which leaps high in the air
at the foot of Kiwanda's cliffs.

Jewell Wildlife Meadows at the foot of
Saddle Mountain in the Coast Range. Here
the State Game Commission purchased
farmland where visitors are afforded an
opportunity to view deer and large herds of
elk when winter snow in higher elevations
forces the animals to lower pastures.

Yaquina Light is viewed for many miles
from the coast highway, where it parallels
surf-washed beaches.

A coastal sunset is a sight to behold but
none can be enjoyed with a more spectacular
and famous setting than at Cannon Beach
where Haystack Rock and The Needles stand
in bold silhouette against the glowing sky.

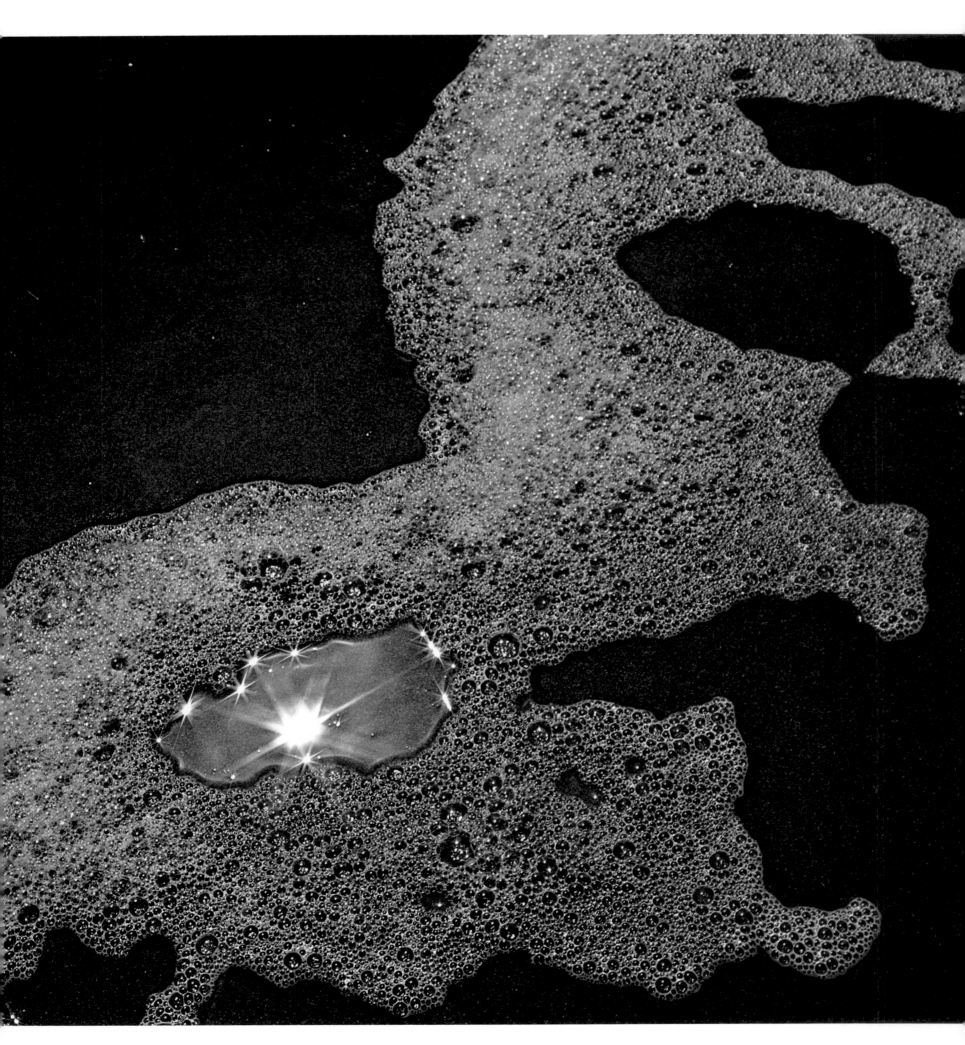

Gentle waves leave interesting patterns of
foaming bubbles that slowly disappear as
if by magic.

Sea foam often rolls up on sandy beaches
during exciting surf action.

A Kiwanda dory breasts an incoming
breaker as fishermen leave the beach at Pacific City
for a day of offshore salmon fishing.

Dories race back to shore ahead of an
approaching weather front.

A spectacular explosion of foaming surf
results when a large breaker crashes against
an offshore rock near Rocky Creek State Park.

Early morning dew cloaks fairways of
a Lincoln County golf course.

A warm sunny day on the beach at Fogarty
Creek State Park.

A choice location for homes and motels
on the picturesque shoreline beside the
coast highway near Depoe Bay.

Pastel tints of the setting sun and hazy clouds silhouette the largest of two famed "Haystack Rocks" on the Oregon Coast. This one is a mile offshore from Cape Kiwanda. It is a bird sanctuary and a popular rendezvous for offshore fishing.

The Nestucca River estuary is one of several
such estuaries which conservationists are
endeavoring to preserve and protect from
encroachment of civilization's progress. The
sandspits and tide flats are wildlife habitats.

A golf course is draped like a lei around
this coastal community nestled in a grove
of evergreens overlooking the Pacific.

Springtime foliage on moss-draped alder
trees screens a view of Munson Falls in the
western foothills of the Coast Range.

Spindrift sails from big Pacific rollers as they
race shoreward against an offshore breeze.

Sunlight finds its way to the floor of a forest
corridor in the Coast Range where autumn-
tinted foliage contrasts dramatically with
deep shadows of evergreen giants.

A sandspit reaches out into the Salmon
River estuary from rugged headlands and
picturesque beaches.

The lava-bound coastline of Rocky Creek
State Park is lashed by explosive breakers.

Scalloped sandstone cliffs and rough surf
combine to create a picturesque waterfall as
a huge wave cascades back into the sea.

A few bushes of scotch broom transplanted from Europe started a golden wave that spread all over the coastal area and much of the Pacific Northwest.

Evergreen trees twisted and contorted into
unusual shapes in a coastal rain forest.

Newport harbor is a haven for one of the
busiest fishing fleets on the Pacific Coast.

THE CENTRAL COAST

All through the long afternoon shouts and laughter drifted across Cleawox Lake from the mountainous sand dune that sweeps sharply up from the warm water. Children struggled to the crest, then turned and rolled or ran down, hitting the water with a noisy splash to wash off the fine grains of sand.

Then, as the afternoon reddened into evening, the noise stopped and in groups of three and four, adults joined the children on the dunes and stood silently gazing toward the west. It was as though a band of ancient sun worshippers had gathered to watch their god leave the day. As the light failed, the groups began slowly leaving the dune, and the sound of automobile doors slamming and grinding starters filtered through the tall rhododendrons, azaleas, coast huckleberries and salal that surround each picnic site. Another day in Jesse Honeyman State Park had ended.

Those vast, rolling dunes are the dominant feature of the central coast, and one does not mention the 50-mile stretch of shoreline from Heceta Head to Coos Bay without thinking of them. Rolled up on the beach from sandstone deposits on the continental shelf, and down to the sea from the Coast Range, then moved about and shaped by the wind, the dunes sometimes reach 400 feet in height.

The individual grains of sand have been rounded by their travels so that they can never pack tightly. Consequently, the dunes are excellent for water storage and hold enough in streams and lakes both above and below ground to support 18 commercial and domestic wells in the Coos Bay-North Bend area alone. One well provides the water supply for the Menasha paper mill at North Bend. The Forest Service, which manages most of the dunes area, keeps a close watch on the water level with numerous test wells lest too much water be pumped out, permitting saltwater to creep inland through the sand. Except for the Jesse Honeyman State Park, a cranberry bog and a scattering of public and privately owned land on the edges of the dunes, they are under Forest Service supervision.

Numerous efforts have been made in the past to establish a national park, and it is obvious that a governmental agency must control the dunes with recreation as their primary use. The latest effort has been by the Forest Service. Dune buggies are increasing in number—nearly 500 using the dunes at the latest count—and regulations must be both established and enforced.

Some dune stabilization has been undertaken by the Forest Service by planting scotch broom and European beach grass in areas where the sand threatens Cleawox Lake, Highway 101 and the Siuslaw River estuary.

No matter how one decides to explore the dunes, it is a fascinating way to spend a day or two. At both Florence and Hauser tours on large-wheeled buggies are available at reasonable prices. Another excellent way is to rent horses and ride through the stubborn forests which cling precariously to life in the hostile environment. Trees that once were 50 feet or higher now are submerged with only their tops showing, and those on the edges of the dunes may be taller, but their new growth has been sandblasted away, leaving only a fringe of green showing at the top.

Although it sounds almost absurd, the dunes are famous for the lakes in and around them, ranging from the large Woahink and Cleawox to tiny, damp depressions formed as enough sand slowly accumulated to dam streams. A few deer and raccoons still live on the islands of trees and berries standing above the rippling and rolling sand, and the small drinking holes preserve their hoof and paw prints throughout the day. Like all wildlife near areas of intense use, their numbers are declining.

Not all this stretch of coastline is barren. Another geologic feature set apart by natural forces is Cape Perpetua, one of the Forest Service's most tastefully and completely developed recreational areas in the Siuslaw National Forest. At this rugged promontory it is possible to learn in a very short time the tenuous relationship between wind, sea, plants, wildlife and man.

Discovered and named by Captain Cook on Saint Perpetua's Day in 1778, it was formed by a series of lava flows which cooled and hardened as the molten rock hit the water. A crack developed in the rock, creating Devil's Churn, a fissure that reaches back beneath the mountainside. It is an area of wild surfs, even on relatively calm days and a place one can be sure of taking photos of waves exploding on the shore.

The Forest Service has self-guided nature tours of the cape with tape-recorded lectures on its natural history. For example, here you find that coastal trees are shaped by the wind because the buds on the windward side are dried and killed; hence, only the branches on the lee side grow, giving the trees the contorted shape associated with the coast. Here is a wide variety of intertidal plant and animal life; starfish, anemones, barnacles, mussels, chitons, all live in the basaltic tidepools.

Above the highway on the high bluff overlooking the cape is the visitors' center with displays vividly explaining natural history of the coastline and films and slide shows on the coastal wildlife. Higher still is an observatory with a view of several miles of coastline, often obscured by clouds created as the warm, moist ocean wind sweeps upward to the cooler land mass.

While this section of coast isn't so intensely developed and populated as the northern stretch, it is an area of heavy recreational use. It is particularly popular with fishermen. When the salmon are running, Yaquina Bay, Alsea Bay at Waldport, Winchester Bay at Reedsport and Coos Bay are major avenues of departure for the open ocean. At other times, Woahink, Siltcoos, Tahkenitch, Clear, Eel and the many-fingered Tenmile Lake have excellent fishing. The larger lakes empty into the ocean and support heavy runs of coho salmon.

It is an adventure to park and dart across Highway 101, but once visitors to the Sea Lion Caves enter the elevator that drops 208 feet through the cliff, the "another world" feeling takes over. The caves offer an amphitheater view of what is believed to be the only sea lion rookery on the U. S. mainland. They are properly called Stellar sea lions in honor of the German naturalist who accompanied Vitus Bering on his second voyage of discovery from Russia to Alaska in 1714.

The cave, a high, vaulted T-shaped cavern with two openings to the sea, is one of the few private businesses operating on the ocean's edge (another is at Otter Crest Wayside, a gift shop operated by the donor of the land). The heavy, lumbering mammals fluctuate their residence in the caves, sometimes alarming naturalists by their absence for a few days when their population is lower than normal during a season. Thus far they have eventually returned, apparently unconcerned with the thousands of people who descend into the cave to gaze at them.

People, obviously, are one of the principal problems faced by agencies charged with managing the coastal resources. Even when people consciously avoid causing damage to the natural surroundings, areas of intense use are the most beautiful or have the most potential for industrial sites. The destruction of these areas comes gradually and has followed a definite pattern here as elsewhere in this growth-oriented, restless nation.

Settlement and exploitation of natural resources have been wedded in our history. Like a bureaucracy, companies, towns and whole industries are based on the assumption that they must grow or they will wither and die. This attitude, still favored by many, has during the past decade started weakening. Belching smokestacks, flues and steam vents on mills have fallen from public favor. Clean, odorless air and undisturbed nature have replaced industrial growth on the priority list.

The 75-square-mile Coos Bay estuary has suffered more from the American growth ethic than any other estuary on the Oregon Coast. A magnificent example of an estuary, it has numerous sloughs, channels, vast salt marshes and rippled mudflats that are a visual delight when the sun glints across them at low tide.

The five-town complex around the bay supports more than 20,000 persons, most of whom depend on the bay industries of logging, shipping and fishing for their income. The estuary suffers on a mathematical basis with the increase in population, and different types of industries compete for control of the bay—farmers, fishermen, recreational interests and finally the large industrialists.

A crash program to save the bay began in the late 1960s and a series of studies and conferences were instigated by the University of Oregon, which has a research center at Charleston; the Oregon State University, the National Park Service and other public and private agencies. The findings invariably were the same: Coos Bay is in the throes of an ecological crisis and all who are dependent on it will suffer unless it is corrected. The reports agreed that industrial and domestic pollution should be kept from the bay, zoning laws with definite land-use guidelines were needed immediately and more aesthetic matters such as billboard control were recommended.

Yaquina Bay proved it is possible to conduct commerce on an estuary without destroying it or driving out other unrelated industries. If the recommendations are followed, Coos Bay, too, will become what it once was—a broad, clean expanse of tidewater where commercial fishing boats and speedboats with water skiers can coexist, where clams can be dug in pure water and where logs no longer will be stored.

While Coos Bay has been a troubled part of the coast, such areas remain the exception. The average tourist is made unaware of major problems because protected land still outweighs the endangered sections.

There is so much land preserved for public use and enjoyment that visitors to the coast with a limited amount of time often find it a frustrating experience; there is simply too much to see and do. There are agates and jasper to look for, silver smelt to dip in huge nets when they're running at Yachats, storms to watch while sitting beside a roaring fireplace in a motel, beaches to hike after the storm in search of Japanese fish-net floats, tide pools to explore and photograph during low tide, fog to walk through when it mutes the colors and hides the offshore rocks.

It is frustrating, but a frustration born of love and anticipation rather than rejection; a frustration that makes tomorrow or next year an event worth living for.

Hundreds of seagulls soar and dive
above a small seashore stream when small fish
leave the Pacific surf to enter fresh water.

A small foothill stream races down a rocky
corridor decorated by golden leaves of native
maple in the autumn season.

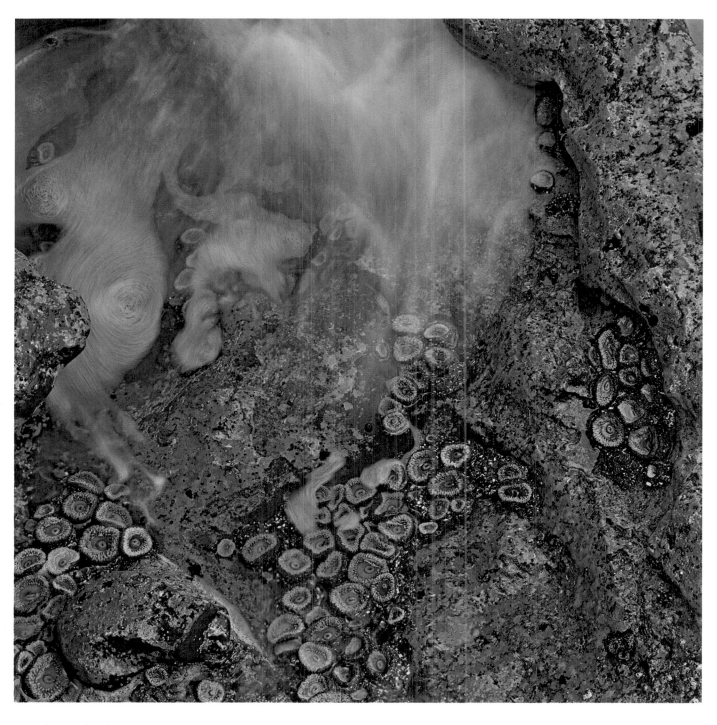

Foaming surf swirls into a tidal pool home
of sea anemone.

The quaint village of Yachats (pronounced
Ya-hots) hugs the shoreline where the Yachats
River meets the Pacific surf.

Summer fun and excitement is the order
of the day when silver smelt runs occur on
the "salt and pepper sand" beach at Yachats.
Several big runs come in on an indefinite
schedule each summer.

Autumn fog melts in morning sunlight to reveal a fairyland picnic setting in a dense forest grove in Neptune State Park.

Cape Perpetua unfurls a grand panorama of the central coast where the mountains rise precipitously from the sea. Several state parks provide exciting shoreline exploring in this area.

State and forest parks in the vicinity of
Cape Perpetua and Devils Churn provide
unexcelled vantage points for surf watching
with each change in mood of the sea.

Thousands of cormorants nest on precipitous
cliffs above the Pacific surf in the vicinity
of the Sea Lion Caves

The great amphitheatre of the Sea Lion
Caves echoes to the roar of the surf. Visitors
may enjoy intimate views of hundreds of
these mammals that claim this as their
year-round domain.

Stonecrop colors rocky cliffs and ledges
all along the coast.

Heceta Light beams its warning to ships at
sea from its perch on a promontory of Heceta
Head above Devils Elbow State Park.

Wild rhododendron and scotch broom
blossoms mingle with colorful foliage of
coast huckleberry among shore pine in
Sutton Lake forest camp.

Wild rhododendron stages the most
spectacular floral show of springtime along
the Oregon Coast where it blooms in
colorful profusion.

76

A constant struggle for life is waged by
pine trees in the shifting coastal sand dunes.
Abundant subsurface moisture encourages
new growth in some areas as the dunes shift
and claim their toll elsewhere.

Forest-bound Siltcoos Lake, one of many
popular fishing and boating havens along
the central coast, contrasts drastically with
vast areas of desert-like sand dunes that
separate the lakes from the sea.

Meadows of golden buttercups border
tideland streams and Darlingtonia or
flycatcher plants thrive in boggy areas
along the central coast.

Indian summer haze veils a swamp-like
lakelet near the seashore.

Fishermen leisurely troll tranquil waters
in a picturesque autumn setting where Pacific
tides have slowed the flow of the Umpqua
River as it finds its way through the Coast
Range.

Vast areas of undulating coastal sand dunes
are a playground for dune buggy enthusiasts.

Oregon's coastal sand dunes are unique
in character and vast in size. Here a seemingly
unlimited reservoir of subsurface water
forms beautiful pools in low areas and gives
life to islands of trees and other vegetation.

Throngs of vacationers enjoy the sand
slopes above Cleawox Lake in Honeyman
State Park.

Gracefully swaying columbine and lush green
maidenhair fern show their appreciation
for shadowed canyon environment and
abundant moisture of Golden and Silver
Falls State Park in western foothills of the
Coast Range.

Dramatic contrasts abound along the Oregon
Coast. Here lush green grass flourishes with
roots below the waters of the Millicoma River
and only a few miles away beach grass seems
just as happy in its wind-swept sand dune
habitat.

A page from the past is this precarious narrow road that only a few years ago gave motorists a grandstand view of Golden Falls. The road is now a path for hikers.

Silver Falls pours over a dome of stone and spreads like a bridal veil as it plunges into the depths of Golden and Silver Falls State Park on the western slope of the Coast Range.

Sword fern reach from the forest floor in the
Coast Range where autumn tinted vine
maple foilage creates a delightful contrast
of natural beauty.

THE SOUTHERN COAST

It was like watching elapsed-time photography, but rather than a flower opening to the spring sun, it was the birth of clouds at Cape Sebastian. It was a brilliant, sunny day with a warm onshore wind blowing and one could watch its movement as it struck the cliffs of Cape Sebastian and deflected upward. When it reached a certain altitude, a cooler zone, streamers of clouds appeared as though a magician were pulling them out of the air, swiftly flying up the mountainside and sweeping over the top, gathering bulk as they progressed.

Many times that morning the cape was completely fogged in and one could only listen to the sea far below and suppose the other point of the cape was still there. Then, the clouds would part, still covering the saddle between the cape's two high points, but letting the sun bathe both points in soft, warm light. Most of the beach was obscured by the fog, but up in the gently sloping hills to the east the fog was rapidly burned off by the sun, giving the green and brown hills a subdued, mottled effect.

The southern coast, from Cape Arago to the California border, takes on a still different set of characteristics. The offshore rocks and the broad, sandy beaches and gentle streams are still there, but back of the beach the land opens up to show hillsides barren of tall forests. Sheep graze along the winding and dipping highway and one is reminded of the Irish and Scottish coastlines.

One soon gets the feeling that this final, fantastically beautiful stretch of coast has not yet become "commercial," that its residents live more in peace with the land. While the southern coast gets its share of the tourist dollar, there is a prevailing attitude perhaps best summed up by a Gold Beach resident:

"Sure, we know the value of tourism, but we've seen what can happen when you try too hard for it. We're trying to find more ways to attract tourists, primarily during the off season, but we're not going to ruin the coast doing it. We like it the way it looks now."

Curry County, which controls most of the southern coast, has conducted numerous studies and set up citizens' committees to both attract new industries and to preserve the natural beauty of the area. It is one of the first counties to see the advantages of advertising the off-season attractions while other areas for years have refused to admit publicly that it frequently rains on the coast, that savage winter storms rake the shoreline or that any part of the year other than the traditional three months of summer are suitable for visiting the beaches.

Residents of the coastal communities have known for dec-

ades that some of the most beautiful weather occurs in the spring and autumn, and only in recent years have motels and chambers of commerce begun advertising the joys of coming to the beach to watch winter storms from the safety and comfort of motel rooms. Rather than attempting to advertise the Northwest shoreline on the basis of a California or Caribbean beach, they have begun selling it for what it really is—a coastline as beautiful as any in the world, but beautiful in its own way. Storms, fog, high winds, crisp mornings, cold water and infrequent hot still days are part of the Northwest Coast heritage. To admit or publicize otherwise is deceitful and a mistake.

A jutting promontory a few miles south of Coos Bay has one of the coast's most dramatic state park complexes. Here at Cape Arago and Shore Acres State Parks the tortured earth is thrust upward, forming sandstone ridges and bluffs for the sea to carve in intricate and bold patterns. The sea, never placid here, constantly crashes over the reefs at the bottom of the cliffs, curls through seahorns it has cut out for itself, shishes as it slides over the rippled and fluted sandstone. Picnic tables are placed like box seats at an opera house for nature, and below hikers often find fossils of sea life that lived millions of years ago.

Both parks were formerly the estate of the Simpson shipbuilding and lumbering family. Cape Arago was donated to the state, and Shore Acres sold along with the intricate formal gardens, still maintained, with rare plants from across the globe. Offshore several hundred yards is the Simpson Reef, a beautiful sight no matter how calm or stormy the sea. On calm days, sea lions frequently bask on the reef, sometimes covered by an unusually large wave, which they ignore.

(There is an old chestnut popular along the coast that should be remembered: "There's always one wave larger than the rest." Generally speaking, waves come from three directions to the shore—southwest, west and northwest. Usually they are out of step and arrive separately. But when waves from two directions meet offshore and join forces, the resulting energy hurls the wave high upon the beach. It is these waves that have swept people off rocks or hurled logs on them. Obviously it is wise to keep a close watch on the surf.)

Not all the Cape Arago park complex is so rugged in its beauty. Sunset Bay is the opposite, calm with a broad crescent-shaped sheltered beach. Behind the beach and across the highway is one of the state's most striking campgrounds, each offering complete privacy from the other by dense and tall screens of coastal plants.

Perhaps more than the rest of the coast, the towns along

this stretch have had more than their share of tragedy, especially in the case of Bandon, a rather scattered and informal town bordered on the west by the sea with huge pinnacles and flat-topped rocks, and on the north by the calm, picturesque Coquille River with the new and pleasant Bullard's Beach State Park.

Bandon's history of infernos probably explains the reluctance to build all houses and businesses together in the traditional rabbit-warren complexes people so love. The first fire was in 1914, and the second and worst in 1936. The town's founder was to blame for the second, and all because he wanted a touch of his homeland in his front yard.

Known as Lord Bennett, he wanted a hedge of gorse, a spiny evergreen shrub similar to scotch broom, and sent to his native Ireland for some seeds. Like so many living imports—English sparrows in this country and rabbits in Australia—the gorse not only survived, it thrived and became a genuine nuisance. Soon it was the dominant shrub throughout the area, and when a forest fire began in 1936, it swept into the gorse and leveled most of Bandon. Its residents could only flee to the beach and watch their town burn.

Gorse still covers much of the land around Bandon and has spread along the western slopes of the Coast Range, although it is unlikely Lord Bennett was responsible for all of it. Today it is controlled by chemicals, reforestation with pine and spruce whose shade keeps it under control, burning and the introduction of its natural enemy from the British Isles, the gorse weevil.

From Bandon the highway swings inland again and doesn't emerge until Port Orford. But Cape Blanco, a high, windswept point with one of the few remaining manned lighthouses on the coast, is a pleasant six-mile side trip worth taking if for no other reason than it is the farthest point west one can drive in the "Lower 48" states. (Cape Alava in Washington is farther west, but is reached only by hiking.)

The cape, which frequently has sheep roaming the steep hills around it, was the first geographic feature in Oregon named by a white man. It was one of the few accomplishments of the Spaniard Martin D'Aguilar, who spotted it in 1603 and named it Blanco (white) for the simple and unromantic reason that its cliffs looked white from the sea. Afternoon tours are offered by the Coast Guard and the view, as one comes to expect in Oregon, is quite spectacular.

Some Northwest coastal Indian tribes were considered "tame" by pioneers, but never the Rogues, as their name would imply. They were fighters for what, with ample justification,

they considered their own. Settlers were unwelcome and none felt less wanted than the group of nine who landed at Port Orford to hunt for gold in 1851. They were stranded on a small island only a few feet offshore and held under siege for several days until they could escape inland to Umpqua and bring reinforcements. Gradually, a policy of extermination was carried out until the last weary survivors of an energetic group of Indians were herded onto reservations. Rockhounds and artifact hunters still stumble onto shell mounds left behind from pre-white man days, and an occasional arrowhead or other archeological records of the original dwellers of this coastline.

Another dweller slaughtered into virtual extinction was the sea otter, but in 1970 a few were reintroduced in the Port Orford area and apparently are thriving on the offshore rocks and sheltered coves.

From Port Orford on is coastal beauty to challenge any other 60-mile stretch in the world. Humbug Mountain State Park has a sheltered area behind its bold cliffs where the wind seldom blows and a beautiful campground near the beach. The drive through the park along Brush Creek is almost startling as one abruptly changes from the open, windswept coast to the quiet, leafy trees growing beside the highway. It is a trait characteristic of the coast that, given a certain amount of protection from the storms, the entire stretch of land from the Coast and Siskiyou Ranges to the beach would be rain forest, and there are numerous spots such as the lee side of Humbug Mountain to prove this assertion.

During the latter half of the 19th Century, gold rushes were almost as common as rock festivals today. Few fortunes were made in Northwest gold rushes, but they did open up new areas for settlement. While some prospectors were stampeding up the Rogue River and into the heart of the Siskiyous, others remained on the coast, hunkered over their pans, working the black sand at the mouth of the Rogue. There was enough gold in the sand to keep a few men there, but not enough to make them wealthy. So they built a town and called it, naturally enough, Gold Beach.

It wasn't gold that kept them there over the years, though. It was, and is, fishing, both commercial and sports; timber, and more recently, tourism. When private planes can safely cross the Siskiyous or fly down the coast, they land at an airstrip only a few steps from the main street. Visitors prospect today for agates and jasper along the beaches or prowl through myrtlewood factories or go on the famous mail boat runs up the swift and rugged Rogue.

Many myrtlewood manufacturers are fond of saying that

the popular wood grows only along the Southern Oregon Coast and in the Holy Land, when in actuality the two trees are not identical. Naturalists classify the Oregon and Northern California myrtle tree as a member of the laurel family. No matter, it is a beautiful wood and rare is the visitor to the coast who does not take or send home a bowl or a bracelet carved and polished from the lustrous wood. In spite of its slow growth and intense harvesting, foresters say the supply is not in danger of depletion, and several groves have been set aside as parks or waysides.

The mail boats run from Gold Beach and its twin city, Wedderburn. They began in 1895 with a man-powered boat making the forty-mile trip up the river to Agness and Illahe as often as the postmaster could row and pole his way back and forth. It is doubtful that Elijah Price and his son, Nobel, ever entertained notions of taking tourists along for the joy of the ride. But today the boats are better known as a tourist diversion than for their primary purpose—delivering mail to residents of the two small towns and other homes along the river.

Reservations are recommended for the boat trips, and some boats don't haul the mail; they load the jet-powered, shallow-draft boats with passengers and go roaring up the Rogue to Agness, where a lunch is served, and return.

Rapids on the river, of which there are many, are called "riffles," and each has its own name, some such as Canfield, Jim Hunt and Gillespie named for people. Others were named for events, such as Coal Riffle where a scow loaded with coal was wrecked. Perhaps the most macabre is "Wake Up Riley Riffle," which earned its named when Judge Riley's partner found gold nearby and came running back into camp yelling, "Wake up, Riley, we've struck it rich!" Poor Riley didn't wake up because he had died in his sleep.

For about 12 miles along the coast north of Brookings the highway climbs and dips and turns along some of the most rough and craggy land on the West Coast. Tiny streams trickle down from the mountains, cross under the highway and empty into the sea. The highway is widened here and punctuated with numerous turnouts. Most of the cliffs are sheer, and only in an occasional cove is it possible to descend to a small beach; an exception is Whales Head Beach, a long, broad stretch of sand beneath the rugged cliffs. Cormorants and pelicans soar between the view points and the ocean below, and seals waddle awkwardly off the rocks and dart gracefully through the water. This is the Samuel H. Boardman State Park, a series of waysides and picnic areas named for perhaps the most important figure in the history of Oregon's state parks.

Usually referred to as the "Father of the Oregon state parks," Boardman was a philosopher, a poet, an engineer, a naturalist and a salesman who could make the wealthy happy to donate park lands and the common man proud of the resulting public property. He believed in making parks represent something other than a pleasant place to stop. "A state rich in historical lore must have its story told within our parks," he said, and that philosophy is reflected in the naming of parks and the plaques they bear somewhere within their boundaries. From his entry into office as first State Parks superintendent in 1929 until his retirement in 1950, the parks had grown from 6,444 acres to 57,195 acres of which 121 parcels ranging up to 5,730 acres were gifts. It is little wonder that his tenure was known as the "acquisition period."

The fifth and final state park with overnight camping facilities open the year around on the coast is Harris Beach. (Others, by the way, are Honeyman, Beverly Beach, Cape Lookout and Fort Stevens.) Harris Beach is a combination of rugged headlands, rocks, dense underbrush of azaleas, salal and poison oak (learn what it looks like and watch for it!) and tidepools literally crowded with starfish, mussels, hermit crabs and agates.

Although Brookings has been through boom-and-bust periods in agriculture, primarily in easter lilies, it has stabilized into a fishing, retirement and lumber town. The unusually mild climate—it is seldom below 50 degrees or above 70—has attracted many retired couples who grow beautiful flowers the year around. On the eastern edge of town is a second state park bordering it, Azalea State Park, which has extremely large native azaleas, some more than 100 years old.

Six miles south and the Oregon Coast joins the California Coast. Except for the agricultural check station, there is little to indicate this voyage of discovery has ended. But it has, and one wonders what part of the coast to select next, what time of year to come. Finally, one wonders how one state could have been so fortunate in selecting leaders decades ago with the foresight to preserve and protect this much nature-in-the-raw for everyone to enjoy always.

We can only hope this assumption is correct; that our grandchildren will be able to peer into a tide pool and watch a starfish slowly move down a barnacle-clad rock and be amazed at the pulsations of a sea anemone and smell only the smells of the shoreline instead of industrial wastes.

This is entirely possible if we take nothing from the seashore and leave only our footprints behind.

Intricate geological patterns of offshore
ledges lashed by foaming surf create a
fascinating sight from the air above Cape
Arago Lighthouse.

Simpson's Reef offshore from Cape Arago
and Shore Acres State Park is the home of
many varieties of marine life, including
sea lions, seals, starfish, anemone, etc. Low
tides permit brief visits by humans who
may enjoy closeup views of marine gardens.
Here, a baby seal seeks warmth of a
small beach of granulated shells.

Shore Acres State Park provides a
grandstand view of varying moods of the sea.
Occasionally gigantic breakers created by
a storm far out on the Pacific explode in
spectacular fury when they crash against reefs
and cliffs.

At times gentle waves wash offshore
ledges of interesting geological design.
On pages 100 and 101 following:
Humbug Mountain scrapes the clouds
high above foaming surf on a rock-studded
sandy beach.

A tiny waterfall tumbles over a sandstone
ledge into a shadowed pool beside a southern
Oregon beach.

Glass floats from Japanese
fishing boats travel for years over several
thousand miles of storm-tossed seas to reach
our Northwest Coast where beachcombers
diligently search for them after each
winter storm.

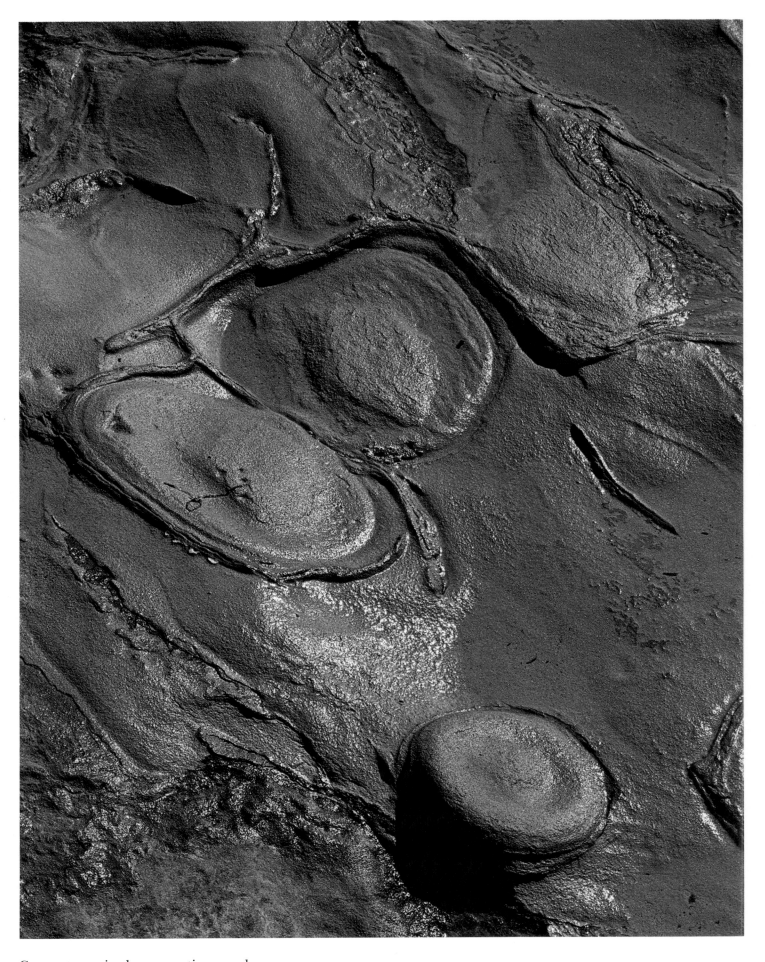

Constant scouring by wave action reveals
unusual geological patterns in sandstone
along the shoreline.

Picturesque old trees cling precariously
to a seashore cliff near Cape Arago where
they have been buffeted by storms.

Scores of rocky pinnacles tower above
extensive areas of sandy beaches at
Bandon.

Wisps of early morning fog veiling
wind-sculptured shoreline trees create an
eerie scene reminiscent of an oriental tapestry.

The coast highway skirts a picturesque
rock-studded beach near Cape Sebastian.

Historic Battle Rock where a small group
of pioneers successfully withstood and
escaped an Indian siege.

Running the wild waters of the Rogue through the Siskiyou Mountains is an adventure of excitement and solitude. Many miles of this famous river can be traveled only by trail or boat.

Several speedy jet boats ply the lower Rogue between Gold Beach and Agness, providing opportunities for hundreds of people to enjoy the beauty of this section of the famous river.

Madrona trees add a touch of color and
variety to evergreen forests in the coastal
foothills of the Siskiyou Range.

Sheep graze freely in rolling hills and
meadows along the southern coast and
huckleberry foliage adds a splash of color to
the windswept hillsides of Cape Sebastian
State Park.

Flowering lupine blankets roadside meadows
in Samuel H. Boardman State Park. Various
shades of blue predominate, however other
colors often add their special touch of beauty
to the mosaic pattern.

Magnificent views of rugged headlands and offshore rocks reward hikers who explore the varied interests revealed from the Indian Sands Trail in Boardman State Park.

Early morning on Whales Head Beach in
Boardman State Park.

A memorial plaque honoring the memory of
Samuel H. Boardman "Father of Oregon State
Parks" has been appropriately located on this
promontory overlooking the Pacific and a large
area of the Park which is traversed by the
Coast Highway for nearly ten miles.

Wild Iris bloom in profusion along
the coast. This delicately tinted variety is
found in the foothills of the Siskiyous
on South Fork of the Coquille River.
Wild Azalea is the show flower of the
southern Oregon coast. In Azalea State
Park, other vegetation has been cleared
so that hundreds of aged shrubs are
displayed at their colorful best.

A somber mood prevails when the setting
sun becomes veiled by an approaching
storm front off the southern coast.

Countless offshore rocks along the southern
Oregon Coast near Harris Beach State Park
are silhouetted by the glow of the setting sun.

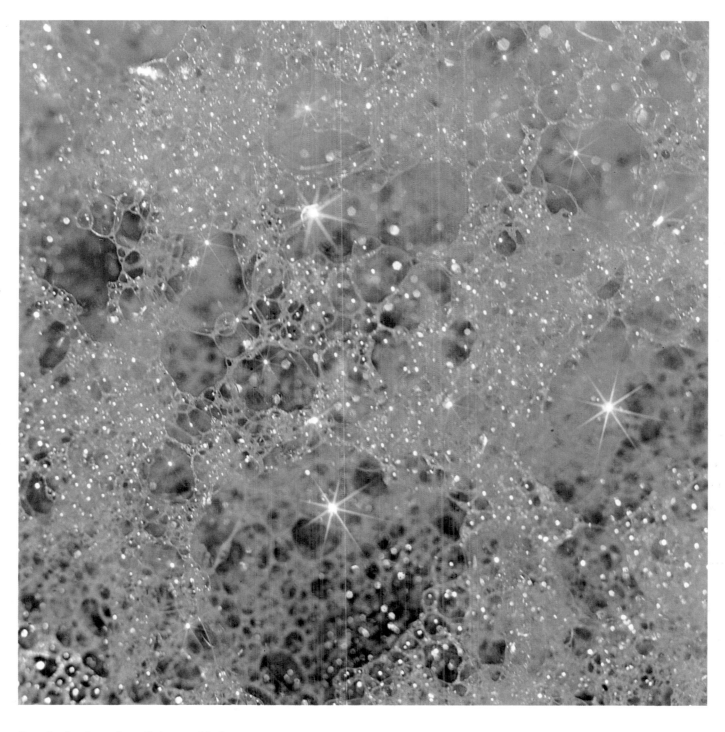

Jewels of reflected sunlight sparkle from bubbles in sea foam left on the beach by a receding wave.

EPILOGUE

Oregon newspapers frequently carry stories and photo essays about the planning problems on the coast. It is the usual confrontation between "bird watchers," some of whom do not live on the coast, and advocates of land development, many of whom do live on the coast. Caught in the middle, as usual, are the county planners trying to perform the impossible task of pleasing everyone. Although neither faction will admit it publicly, compromise is inevitable. It isn't a question of if the appearance of the coast will change, but of where, when and how much.

While the battle was being fought in committee rooms in Washington, D. C., newspaper offices in Portland, on street corners in Lincoln City and restaurants in Tillamook, a family was on its last day of vacation on the coast. A child stood beside her father on a high point, peering through the heavy cyclone fence at the panorama stretching from the northern to the southern horizon. Perhaps remembering what she had been told about fences and cages in zoos, she asked:

"Is it to keep us from hurting the beach?"

"Partly, I suppose," the father replied, an unpleasant glimpse into what could be the future flitting through his mind.

"They won't put a fence around the whole beach, will they?"

"Of course not," the father answered.

But that winter, when one of the children mentioned the nifty agates picked up the previous summer on the Oregon beaches, that fence, erected for safety rather than exclusion, always returned to the father's mind; and that one poignant, childish question:

"They won't put a fence around the whole beach will they?"